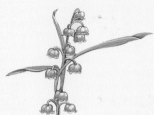

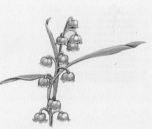

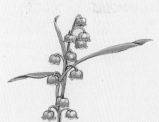
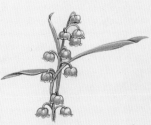

Here Come the BRIDES

ELLEN JACKSON

Illustrations by
CAROL HEYER

Walker and Company
New York

First published in the United States of America in 1998 by Walker Publishing Company, Inc.

Published simultaneously in Canada by Thomas Allen & Son Canada, Limited, Markham, Ontario.

Library of Congress Cataloging-in-Publication Data
Jackson, Ellen B., 1943-
    Here come the brides/Ellen Jackson: illustrated by Carol Heyer.
    p. cm.
    Includes bibliographical references.
    Summary: Describes the customs and traditions connected with weddings all over the world.
    ISBN 0-8027-8468-2 (hardcover). —ISBN 0-8027-8469-0 (reinforced)
    1. Marriage customs and rites—cross-cultural studies—Juvenile literature.
    2. Wedding costume—Cross-cultural studies—Juvenile literature. [1. Marriage customs and rites. 2. Weddings.] I. Heyer, Carol, 1950-ill. II.Title.
    GT2665.J33 1998
    392.5—dc21   97-34857
                                                                            CIP
                                                                            AC

Carol Heyer would like to thank the following models/friends for helping her with this project: Suzan Davis Atkinson, Nick Loughridge, Stephanie Sumell, and Taryn Clyburn.

Book design by Rosanne Kakos-Main

Printed in Hong Kong

10 9 8 7 6 5 4 3 2 1

To my wonderful editors, Emily Easton,
Robin Friedman, and Soyung Pak.
—E. J.

In remembrance of my parents, William J.
and Merlyn Heyer, now and always.
—Lovingly, C. A.

Here Come the Brides

Today, all around the world, men and women begin their marriages with a wedding. A wedding is a time for celebration, a time when a bride and groom pledge their love and loyalty to each other in the presence of friends and family. Everyone shares in the joy of this wonderful, happy occasion.

In the United States, many young girls look forward to a romantic wedding with bridesmaids and a white gown. In other countries, such as Morocco and China, weddings are based on colorful traditions that have stayed the same for hundreds of years.

Wherever a wedding occurs, the bride is at the center of the celebration. She might be young or old. She might be American, Japanese, or Nigerian. She might be getting married in a solemn cathedral or in a farmer's field. Whoever she is, the bride reminds everyone of love and the hope of happiness.

*I*n colonial times, a woman received a wedding thimble when she became engaged. After the marriage, the rim of the thimble was cut off and became the wedding ring.

*O*ne hundred years ago, a Hopi girl would send cornmeal biscuits to the young man she wished to marry. If he ate the biscuits, the couple was engaged.

DID YOU KNOW...

*I*N THE SIXTEENTH AND SEVENTEENTH CENTURIES, SOME ENGLISH LADIES WORE THEIR WEDDING RINGS ON THEIR THUMBS.

*T*he earliest engagement rings were made of grass or rope.

*T*oday when a couple becomes engaged, the man may give his bride-to-be an engagement ring, often a sparkling diamond.

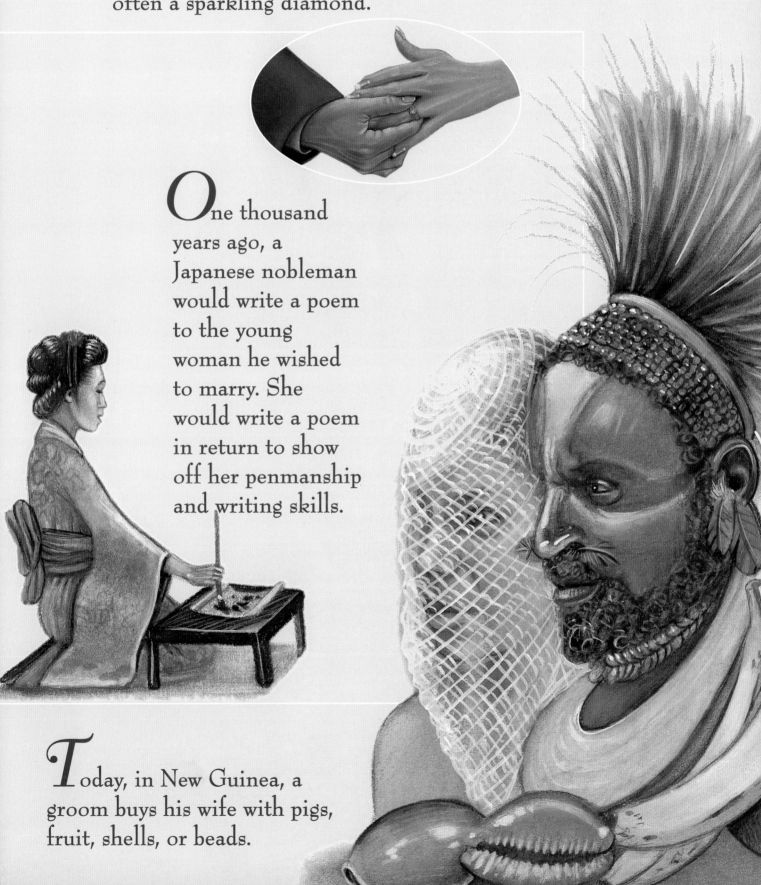

*O*ne thousand years ago, a Japanese nobleman would write a poem to the young woman he wished to marry. She would write a poem in return to show off her penmanship and writing skills.

*T*oday, in New Guinea, a groom buys his wife with pigs, fruit, shells, or beads.

All Dressed In...

ONE OF THE FIRST THINGS an engaged woman does is select a special dress for her special day. She might buy a gown, have one made, or sew it herself. In the United States, a modern bride might choose a dress of lace, silk, or satin. The gown may be hand-embroidered with a full skirt or have simple lines and be worn with a headpiece, such as a tiara. A formal gown often has a train, a part of the dress that trails behind the bride as she walks. Usually, a wedding gown is white if the bride has not been married before.

You may be surprised to learn that wedding gowns are a recent tradition in the West. Until the nineteenth century, a bride in America or Europe wore her best dress during the wedding ceremony no matter what color it was. Even today, wedding gowns come in a rainbow of colors. Whatever dress she wears, the bride wants to look her best on her wedding day.

A Malay bride wears a dress made from songket, a handwoven cloth interwoven with gold thread. The dress can be any color.

DID YOU KNOW...

*A*N OLD SUPERSTITION STATES THAT IF THERE IS A CAT IN THE HOUSE, A BRIDE MUST FEED THE ANIMAL HERSELF ON HER WEDDING DAY OR IT WILL RAIN.

A Spanish bride sometimes wears a traditional black dress and a mantilla, a light scarf worn over the head and shoulders.

*I*n eighteenth-century Italy, wealthy brides wore silk dresses embroidered with gold or silver thread.

*D*uring the Middle Ages, a Jewish bride in the Orient dressed as a man, putting on a helmet and sword.

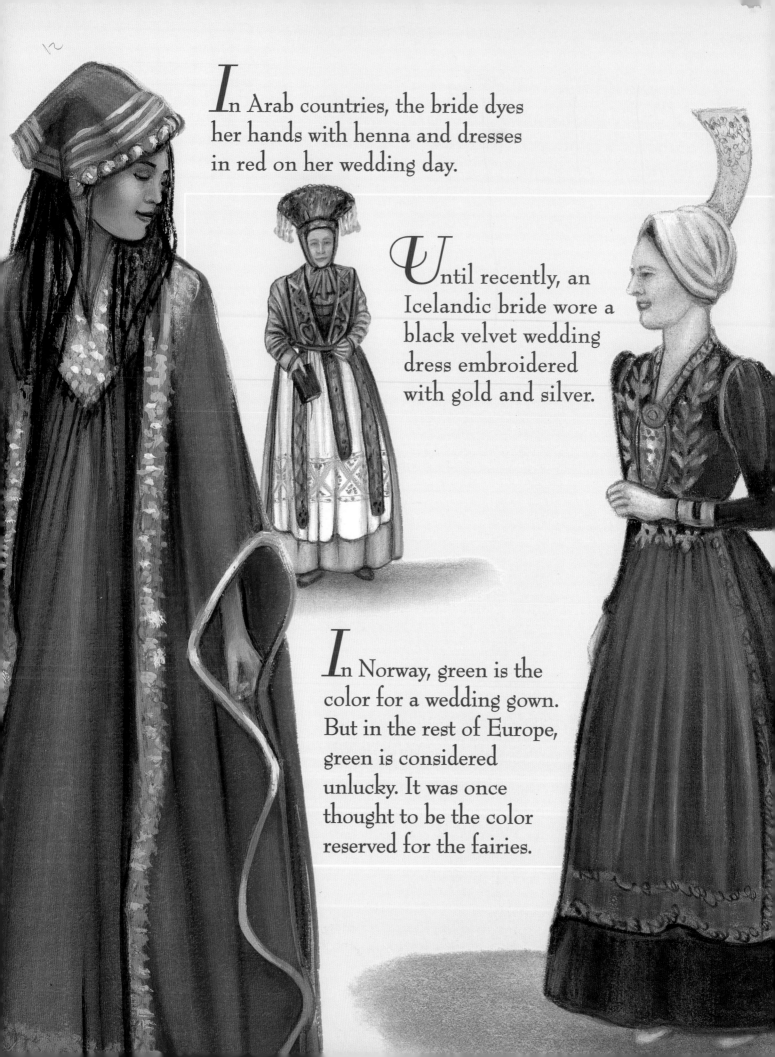

*I*n Arab countries, the bride dyes her hands with henna and dresses in red on her wedding day.

*U*ntil recently, an Icelandic bride wore a black velvet wedding dress embroidered with gold and silver.

*I*n Norway, green is the color for a wedding gown. But in the rest of Europe, green is considered unlucky. It was once thought to be the color reserved for the fairies.

A young Saburu woman from East Africa wears a brightly colored garment and layers of beaded necklaces.

A Quaker bride in 1800 wore a tan taffeta dress with a simple white shawl and a matching bonnet.

DID YOU KNOW...

WHEN QUEEN ELIZABETH OF ENGLAND MARRIED PRINCE PHILIP IN 1947, THEIR WEDDING CAKE WAS NINE FEET TALL AND WEIGHED FIVE HUNDRED POUNDS.

Hair and Makeup

ON HER WEDDING DAY, a bride may have her hair styled or plaited with flowers, or she may wear special makeup or jewelry. She wants to look her best as she enters into her new life with her husband.

During the wedding ceremony, a bride may choose to display her face or hide it behind a veil. The original purpose of the wedding veil was to conceal the bride from evil spirits who might do her harm.

Modern veils are often gauzy and transparent. At the end of the ceremony, the groom lifts the veil and kisses his new wife.

One thing is certain. With or without a veil, and no matter which hairstyle and makeup she chooses, a bride is always beautiful.

A young Masai woman
paints her skin and hair with
red ocher.

16

*I*n Tobelo, a village in Indonesia, the bride's face is adorned with white dots.

*I*n Java, the bride wears a headdress of golden leaves and jasmine.

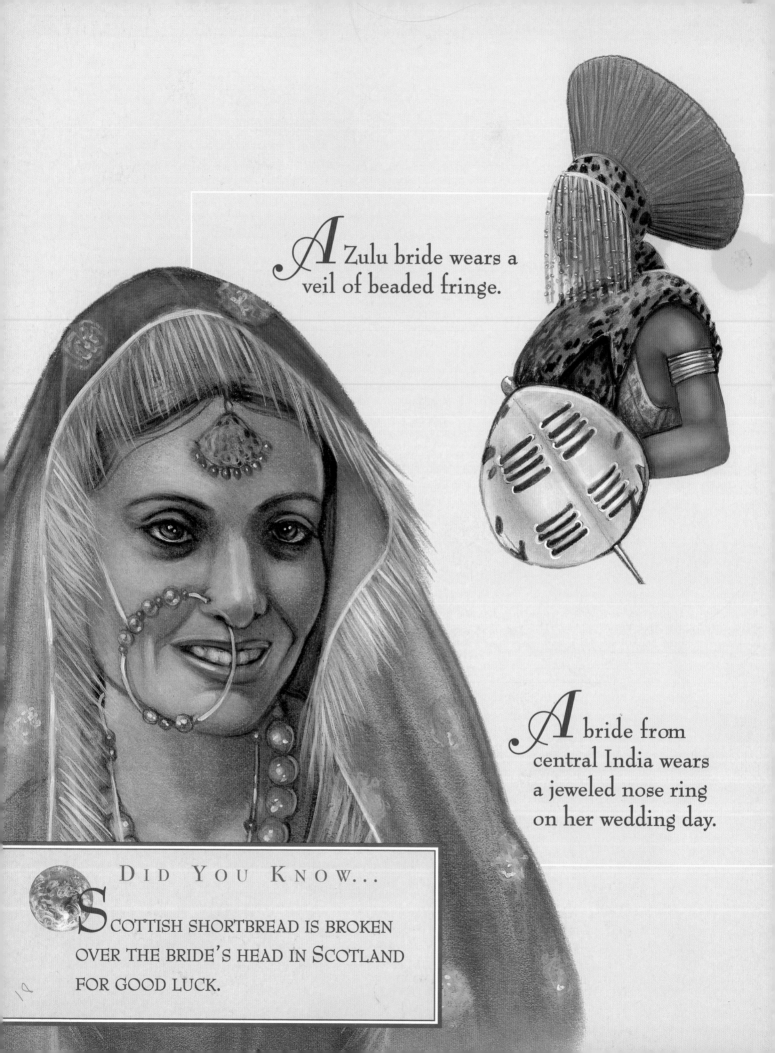

A Zulu bride wears a veil of beaded fringe.

A bride from central India wears a jeweled nose ring on her wedding day.

DID YOU KNOW...

SCOTTISH SHORTBREAD IS BROKEN OVER THE BRIDE'S HEAD IN SCOTLAND FOR GOOD LUCK.

*T*he Korean bride decorates her face with dots made of fabric.

*I*n one South-East Asian tribe, women once wore brass neck rings to ward off evil spirits.

19

Family and Friends

A WEDDING CELEBRATES the coming together of two people—and two families. Friends and family make the wedding more meaningful by sharing their love and support with the couple on their special day. They also help with the details, such as decorating, preparing food, and making toasts to the newlyweds.

Long ago, people believed that evil spirits might try to harm a new bride. It was thought that if the young woman's friends dressed alike, they might fool the evil spirits who would be unable to find the real bride. In modern times, these friends have become bridesmaids, and they are still an important part of a wedding ceremony, along with the ushers and best man, who are friends of the groom.

Children have always been a part of wedding ceremonies, too. In the past, people thought that the presence of children would bring good luck and help the couple have many children of their own. Today, the flower girl and ring bearer represent the couple's hope for the future.

When everyone is assembled, the ceremony begins. Then the bride appears and gracefully walks down the aisle with her father—or in Jewish weddings with both parents—to take her place beside the groom.

*I*n Switzerland, bridesmaids throw colored handkerchiefs at the guests. Those who catch one are expected to give money to the married couple.

*M*others and fathers usually toast the newlyweds. They will do everything they can to help the young couple have a good life together.

*A*n Arab bride may ride to her wedding on a camel. Well-wishers line the road as the procession passes.

In Greece, it is the custom for a country
bride to sit a young boy on her lap and hang
a ring biscuit around his neck.

A flower girl walks
down the aisle, tossing
rose petals to provide a
carpet of flowers for the
bride. The ring bearer
carries the wedding
rings on a pillow.

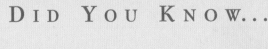

DID YOU KNOW...

AMONG THE IBO PEOPLE OF AFRICA,
A MAN IS SUPPOSED TO HELP HIS FUTURE
FATHER-IN-LAW WITH PLANTING AND
HARVESTING FOR MANY YEARS WHILE HIS
FUTURE BRIDE GROWS FROM A CHILD
INTO A YOUNG WOMAN.

Symbols and Traditions

FROM EARLIEST TIMES, symbols and traditions have been a part of weddings. Everyone wanted to protect the bride and groom and ensure their joyful future together. Special customs developed to express this wish for good luck and happiness.

For example, the bride carries a bouquet of lilacs or roses, or even a basket of wildflowers and herbs. Each herb or flower in the bouquet has a special meaning. Roses stand for love, lilacs for innocence, and rosemary for remembrance. Orange blossoms represent a wish for children. After the ceremony, the bride throws the bouquet. It is said that whoever catches it will be the next to marry.

Another familiar symbol is the wedding ring. Rings are worn because a circle is said to be a symbol of eternity. The modern wedding ring is usually worn on the fourth finger of the left hand. This custom was started by the Egyptians, who believed that a vein ran directly from that finger to the heart.

The food a bride and groom share on their wedding day has special meaning. In the United States, couples share a piece of wedding cake to symbolize the bond that now unites them. This is a tradition that began in ancient Rome. Muslim newlyweds bite into the same piece of candy, and a Japanese bride and groom eat from the same plate of rice.

Everywhere today, these traditions, superstitions, and customs are an important part of a wedding, reminding a bride of the past as she steps into her new life.

26

A Korean bridegroom will ask a happily married friend to make two small wooden ducks as a good luck charm for his new home. In Korea, it is believed that ducks mate for life.

An Anglo-Saxon father would hit his daughter over the head with a shoe to knock the demons out of her before she went off with her new husband.

In Great Britain, it's considered lucky for a black cat to cross the bride's path on her way to the wedding.

DID YOU KNOW...

IF AN UNMARRIED GIRL PUTS A PIECE OF WEDDING CAKE UNDER HER PILLOW, IT IS SAID SHE WILL DREAM OF HER FUTURE HUSBAND.

*I*n Iran, Syria, Turkey, and India, a bride and groom try to step on each other's toes during the ceremony. It is said that the first to do so will be the boss of the marriage.

*I*n medieval times, the bridal bouquet included garlic, bay leaves, chives, and other herbs to scare off evil spirits.

*A*fter the wedding, a Greek bride throws a ripe pomegranate at a door smeared with honey. If seeds stick to the door, people believe that the marriage will be happy and blessed with many children.

A Pledge to the Future

NOT ALL WEDDINGS ARE THE SAME—even in the same country. Although many couples choose to have a traditional wedding, each couple is different. A bride and groom may want a ceremony that reflects their own beliefs, interests, and personalities. They may recite their vows in front of a fireplace while snow falls outside. They may have a small wedding in front of a justice of the peace. Or they may combine elements of various cultures, making their wedding truly special for them.

When the ceremony has ended, there is usually a celebration. This might be a small party for friends or an elaborate reception with an orchestra playing and people dancing beneath crystal chandeliers.

A new life awaits every newlywed couple no matter what kind of wedding they have. Their dreams of the future are just beginning to blossom. But whatever comes next, the bride and groom will never forget their wedding day. It will live in their memories forever.

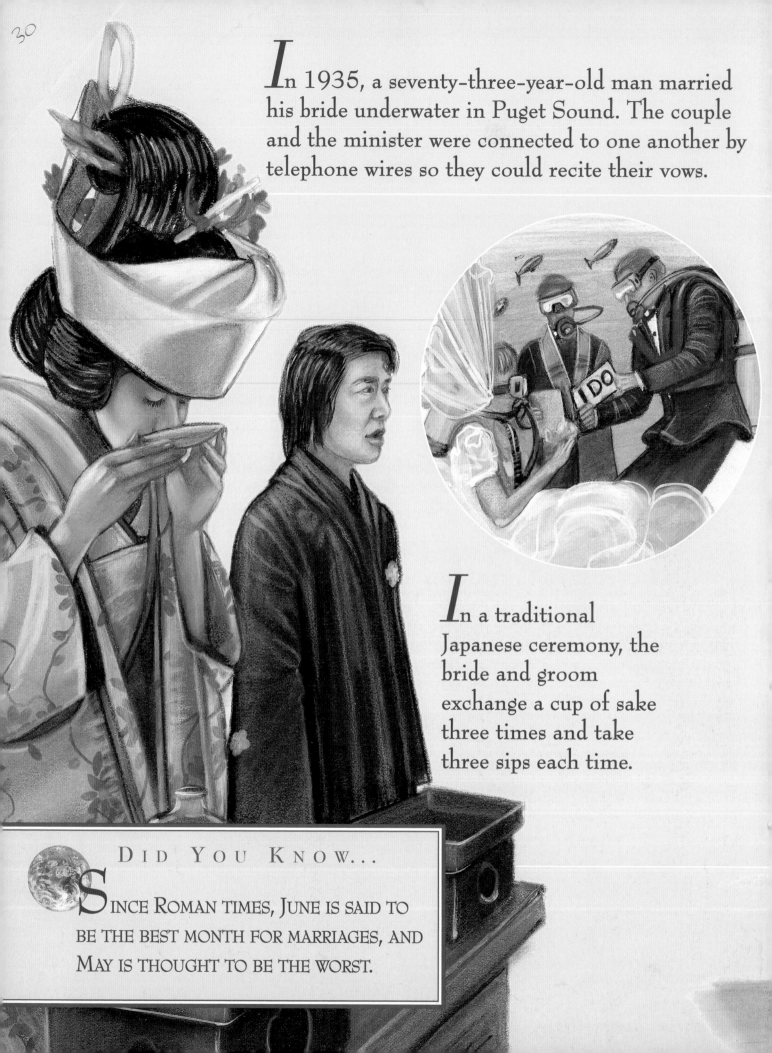

*I*n 1935, a seventy-three-year-old man married his bride underwater in Puget Sound. The couple and the minister were connected to one another by telephone wires so they could recite their vows.

*I*n a traditional Japanese ceremony, the bride and groom exchange a cup of sake three times and take three sips each time.

DID YOU KNOW...

*S*INCE ROMAN TIMES, JUNE IS SAID TO BE THE BEST MONTH FOR MARRIAGES, AND MAY IS THOUGHT TO BE THE WORST.

*I*n a Jewish ceremony, the groom puts the veil on the bride before she walks down the aisle.

*O*n September 5, 1992, a young couple was married on the Grand National roller coaster at Blackpool Pleasure Beach in England.

*B*efore the Civil War, two slaves would marry by jumping over a broom together.

Bibliography

Anastasio, Janet, and Michelle Bevilacqua. *The Everything Wedding Book*. Holbrook, Mass.: Adams Media, 1994.

Jones, Leslie. *Happy Is the Bride the Sun Shines On: Wedding Beliefs, Customs, and Traditions*. Chicago: Contemporary Books, 1995.

Kirschenbaum, Howard, and Rockwell Stensrud. *The Wedding Book*. New York: Seabury Press, 1974.

Lee, Vera. *Something Old, Something New*. Naperville, Ill.: Sourcebooks, 1994.

Metrick, Sydney Barbara. *I Do*. Berkeley: Celestial Arts, 1992.

Murphy, Brian. *The World of Weddings: An Illustrated Celebration*. New York: Paddington Press, 1978.

Seligson, Marcia. *The Eternal Bliss Machine: America's Way of Wedding*. New York: William Morrow, 1973.

Tasman, Alice Lea Mast. *Wedding Album: Customs and Lore Through the Ages*. New York: Walker and Company, 1982.

Tober, Barbara. *The Bride*. New York: Harry N. Abrams, 1984.

Urlin, Ethel Lucy. *A Short History of Marriage*. Detroit: Singing Tree Press, 1969.